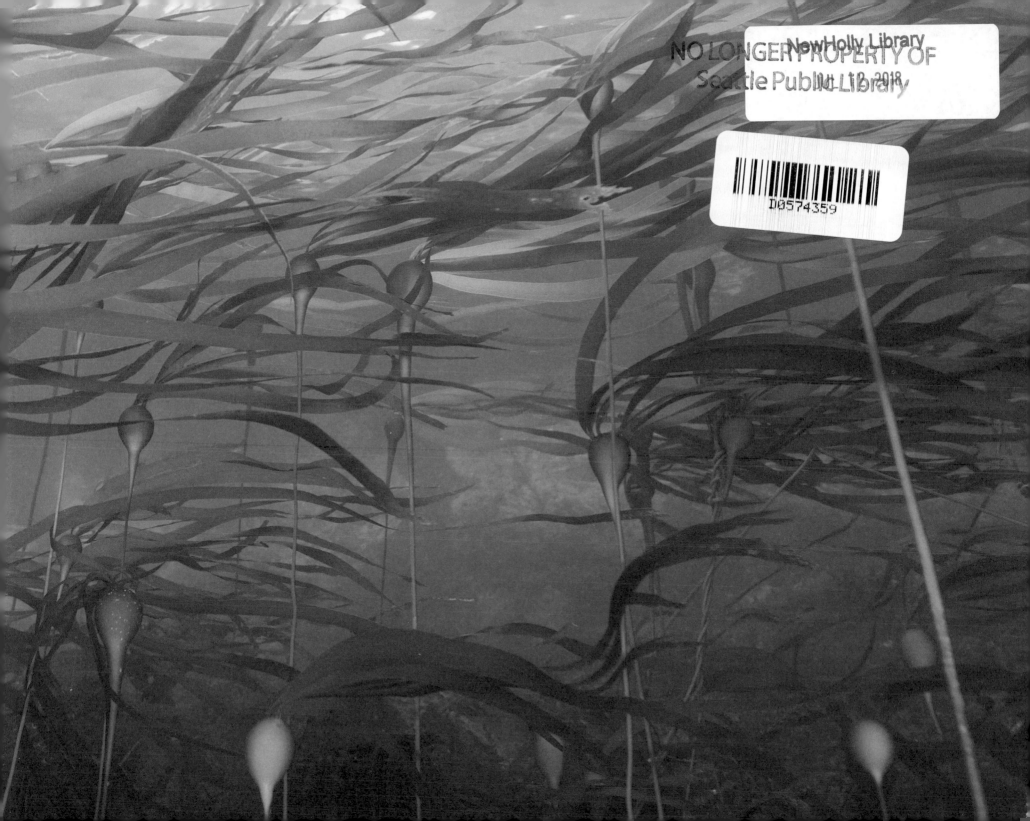

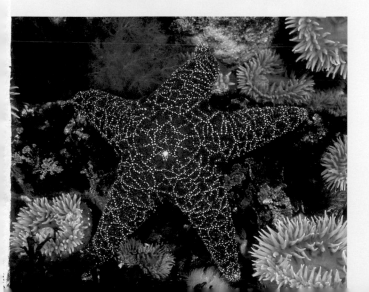

Explore the
Salish Sea

A NATURE GUIDE FOR KIDS

Joseph K. Gaydos, SEADOC SOCIETY, and
Audrey DeLella Benedict, CLOUD RIDGE NATURALISTS

little bigfoot
an imprint of sasquatch books
seattle, wa

Spot prawn

We dedicate this book to the next generation who will inherit the Salish Sea. We hope to inspire you to care for it and hope you will be proud of what we leave you.

Manufactured in China by C&C Offset Printing Co. Ltd. Shenzhen, Guangdong Province, in December 2017

Published by Little Bigfoot, an imprint of Sasquatch Books

22 21 20 19 18   9 8 7 6 5 4 3 2 1

Editor: Christy Cox | Production editor: Em Gale
Design: Bryce de Flamand | Copyeditor: Rachelle Longé McGhee

Front cover photos: Pete Naylor (top left), Drew Collins (top center), Paul Colangelo (top right), Amy Gulick (middle), Craig Weakley (bottom left), Jessica Newley (bottom middle), Brandon Cole (bottom right)
Back cover photo: Brandon Cole
Endsheet photos: Marc Chamberlain (front right), Brandon Cole (front left and back)

ISBN: 978-1-63217-095-8

Sasquatch Books
1904 Third Avenue, Suite 710 | Seattle, WA 98101
(206) 467-4300 | SasquatchBooks.com

Contents

V   **Introduction**
Welcome to the Salish Sea

1   *Chapter 1*
Where Is the Salish Sea?

7   *Chapter 2*
Why the Salish Sea Is Special

13   *Chapter 3*
Beach Stones Have Stories to Tell

21   *Chapter 4*
Life at the Edges:
The Intertidal World

29   *Chapter 5*
Life in the Deep: The Subtidal World

39   *Chapter 6*
Life Between Two Worlds: Diving
Birds and Mammals

45   *Chapter 7*
Epic Journeys

49   *Chapter 8*
Be a Salish Sea Hero

52   **Acknowledgments**

53   **Photo Credits**

54   **Index**

Three different *ecotypes* (or types) of killer whales can be found in the Salish Sea: marine mammal eaters, called transients; salmon eaters, called residents; and shark eaters, called offshores.

WHERE WOULD YOU GO TO SEE the ocean's top hunter, the world's largest octopus, a 95-year-old fish, or a seabird that flies underwater? The Salish Sea.

Killer whales, octopuses, rockfish, and rhinoceros auklets are just the tip of the iceberg when it comes to cool things you can find in the Salish Sea. You don't need to be a scientist or a scuba diver to explore this sea. Join us for a "dive" into these waters, and we will tell you all about how this place came to be home to millions of people and so many fascinating animals.

KILLER WHALE

Killer whales, also known as orcas, are beloved residents of the Salish Sea. These *apex* (or top) predators can weigh up to 21,000 pounds (9,500 kg), which is almost twice as much as an elephant. Their giant interlocking teeth, which are 3 to 4 inches (7.6 to 10.2 cm) long, give them the fearsome look of an aquatic *Tyrannosaurus rex*. Killer whales may seem scary, but these giant predators live in complex societies, hunt cooperatively, share food, help care for each other's young, and show other signs of being highly intelligent.

GIANT PACIFIC OCTOPUS

The giant Pacific octopus is the largest octopus species in the world. In the Salish Sea, adults can tip the scales at 150 pounds (68 kg)!

Octopuses have 8 arms, which they use to swim, explore their surroundings, capture prey, and even place an occasional giant hug on a scuba diver. But these brainy hunters are also "armed" with another weapon: super suckers. Females have a total of 2,240 suckers—280 suckers on each arm. Males have 2,060 because they only have 100 suckers on their third left arm, which they use for transferring sperm to females. Each sucker is a complicated muscle topped with a suction cup, a minibrain control center, and special sensory cells that can "taste" and identify whatever the sucker touches. It's like being able to taste with your fingertips—all 2,240 or 2,060 of them!

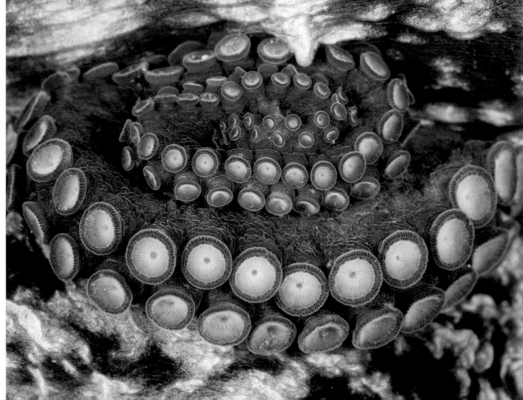

QUILLBACK ROCKFISH

Quillback rockfish are as colorful and beautiful as the reefs they live on. Their name gives them away, however—they're more than just a pretty face. Quillback rockfish are members of the Scorpion-fish family and have venomous spines, or quills, along their backs (called the dorsal fin) that they can pop up in an instant to scare away or even inject venom into predators. With that kind of protection, it's no surprise quillback rockfish can live to the ripe old age of 95 years!

In the Salish Sea, quillback rockfish like these are homebodies. Once they are adults, they may live their entire lives within 100 square feet (10 square m). And if you try to trick one by moving it to a new area, it will just return to its old home (so don't bother trying).

RHINOCEROS AUKLET

Rhinoceros auklets are named for the rhinoceros-like "horn" that sticks up from the top of their orange beak. These birds are excellent swimmers, using their powerful wings to "fly" underwater, very similar to how most birds fly through the air. Their finlike wings, waterproof feathers, and webbed feet enable them to make a living catching fish underwater, where they can stay for up to 2½ minutes before needing to take a breath of air.

Check out this auklet (right) with his beak full of fish. Catching the first one might be easy, but how does the auklet catch another without losing the first? Simple! Auklets have tiny barbs (hooks) on the roof of their mouth that keep their catch from escaping while they capture more. Watch closely and you might just see an auklet with as many as thirteen fish in its beak!

A rhinoceros auklet dives (left) and surfaces with a bill full of Pacific sand lance (right) to feed its chick. These birds come to land in the spring to hatch and raise a chick. Instead of building a regular bird's nest, they excavate an underground burrow that can be as long as 15 feet (4.5 m). Parents, cautious of gulls that will try to steal this meal, bring fish back to their chick under the cover of darkness.

The Salish Sea is home to killer whales, giant Pacific octopuses, quillback rockfish, rhinoceros auklets, and thousands of other amazing creatures. Many will be easy to see, while others are more secretive or so small that you'll need to search for them. It's all part of the fun of becoming a nature detective.

THE SALISH SEA BY THE NUMBERS

- Coastline length (including islands): 4,642 miles (7,470 km)

- Total number of islands: 419

- Sea surface area: 6,535 square miles (16,925 square km)

- Maximum sea depth: 2,133 feet (650 m) at Bute Inlet, British Columbia

- Human population: about 8 million

- Number of animal species: 38 mammals, 172 birds, 253 fish, 2 reptiles, and more than 3,000 *macroinvertebrates* (creatures without backbones that you can see without a microscope)

Campbell River, BC

STRAIT OF GEORGIA

Vancouver, BC

VANCOUVER ISLAND

Nanaimo, BC

Bellingham, WA

Port Renfrew, BC

Victoria, BC

STRAIT OF JUAN DE FUCA

OLYMPIC PENINSULA

PUGET SOUND

N

Seattle, WA

Olympia, WA

Chapter 1
Where Is the Salish Sea?

THE SALISH SEA STRADDLES the international border between the United States (Washington State) and Canada (British Columbia), and includes the inland marine waters of the Strait of Juan de Fuca, Puget Sound, and the Strait of Georgia. Salish Sea waters lap against the shores at the southern end of Vancouver Island and surround the San Juan Islands in Washington State, the Gulf Islands in British Columbia, and numerous other islands on both sides of the border (419 islands in all, to be exact!).

How did the Salish Sea get its name? Long before the first European explorers arrived in the Pacific Northwest, Coast Salish people lived along its shores. Today, as in the past, their lives continue to be shaped by the bounty of land and sea. In 2009, this special ecosystem was named to honor these first inhabitants and their descendants who still call the Salish Sea home and help care for this amazing place.

Coast Salish tribes and First Nations still reside along the Salish Sea and are important stewards. Here Tsleil-Waututh, Squamish, Musqueam, and other First Nations protest against the expansion of a crude oil pipeline into their homeland and work to protect the natural resources that are important to all of us.

Compared to the Coast Salish, who have a long history in the region, European explorers came to this region relatively recently—only a few hundred years ago. Many of the place names you see on maps of the Salish Sea, such as Strait of Juan de Fuca, Puget Sound, Vancouver, Fraser River, San Juan Island, and Lopez Island, reflect this European exploration. The name Salish Sea doesn't change any of these names, but for the first time gives one name to the entire sea. How fitting that it honors the region's original inhabitants.

The Salish Sea is one small part of Earth's vast blue oceans that cover over two-thirds of the planet's surface. The dominance of oceans is unique to Earth and is why it's called the "blue planet." This *global ocean* is truly one interconnected body of water made up of five major oceans—the Pacific, Atlantic, Southern (Antarctic), Indian, and Arctic—and many smaller connecting seas, gulfs, and bays.

Why are oceans so important? The global ocean is truly Earth's life-support system. Our oceans are in constant motion, and their swirling currents circle the globe, generating most of our oxygen, absorbing carbon dioxide, regulating temperatures, and determining our climate and weather.

The global ocean is also the "engine" that drives the *water cycle*. Water evaporates from the oceans and becomes water vapor, which travels up into the atmosphere and then returns to land as rain and snow. The water cycle is what makes life on Earth possible. No matter where you live, nearly every drop of water you drink and all the air that you breathe come from the ocean.

The Salish Sea and our global ocean support the greatest abundance and *biodiversity* (or diversity of life) on Earth. Scientists believe that the first forms of life began evolving in oceans nearly 4 billion years ago.

We wouldn't be here without our oceans, and the Salish Sea is just as important to its local inhabitants as the global ocean is to the Earth's entire population.

Every spring, tufted puffins come to the Salish Sea to raise their young. In the fall, they return to the Pacific Ocean. They are one of many species that connect the Salish Sea to the global ocean.

This satellite view of Earth shows that the Salish Sea is a part of the Pacific Ocean—the oldest, largest, and deepest of our planet's oceans. The global ocean contains about 97 percent of all the water on Earth, and the Pacific contains nearly half of that amount.

SALISH SEA

PACIFIC OCEAN

Sucia and the Finger Islands, which are situated near the border between Canada and the United States, are a few of the 419 islands that dot the Salish Sea—but their geologic story is the most fascinating of all the islands.

AN INTERNATIONAL BORDER BISECTS THE SALISH SEA

For the water, fish, and wildlife that move freely throughout the Salish Sea, the international border that divides this ecosystem has no meaning. For us humans, however, it means we have to cooperate with our neighbors when taking care of this special place. Together, the governments of Canada, the United States, and the Coast Salish tribes and First Nations must make decisions on conservation issues. One example is deciding how many salmon should be harvested and how many should be left in the ecosystem.

Chapter 2
Why the Salish Sea Is Special

THE SALISH SEA IS UNIQUE. There is no other place like it on Earth. Oceanographers define the Salish Sea as an *inland sea* because it is largely landlocked. The Strait of Juan de Fuca is the main passageway for saltwater entering the sea from the Pacific Ocean. And the many rivers that flow into it provide a steady source of freshwater, making the Salish Sea an *estuary*, a place where freshwater and saltwater mix.

Because the Salish Sea is an estuary, its boundaries don't stop at the shoreline but extend to the tops of the huge mountain ranges that surround the sea. That's right: the Salish Sea ecosystem includes the forest *as well as* the water! The mountains and forests around the Salish Sea are called *watersheds*. They act like a giant sponge, capturing oxygen-rich freshwater and releasing it into the Salish Sea through a network of streams and rivers.

As you stand in a grove of ancient cedar trees (left), it may be hard to imagine that the Salish Sea ecosystem extends from the lush evergreen forests of the surrounding mountains all the way to these painted anemones on the seafloor (right).

7

Just as mountains and watersheds feed freshwater to the Salish Sea, salmon bring nutrients from the ocean back to the forests. After growing up in the ocean, salmon return to rivers where they spawn and die. Their bodies become food for bears, birds, raccoons, and dozens of other forest animals, and they also provide nutrients for the trees and plants that line the stream. No doubt about it: the sea and the forest are connected!

In contrast to the oxygen-rich freshwater entering the Salish Sea from its watersheds, the saltwater entering through the Strait of Juan de Fuca from the Pacific Ocean is oxygen-poor but very rich in nutrients. This nutrient-rich seawater flows into the Salish Sea far below its surface. The oxygen-rich freshwater that comes from the surrounding mountains is more buoyant and floats on the surface of the seawater as it enters. The combined forces of tides, currents, and wind act like a giant blender, mixing the freshwater and saltwater into a nutritious oxygen-rich "soup" that supports a treasure trove of life.

Look at this satellite image. Can you track the path of Fraser River from the mountains, through the greater Vancouver metropolitan area, and into the Salish Sea? At times, freshwater entering the Salish Sea can be a trickle. Other times it can be a flood. In the summer, after winter snow on the mountains has melted and filled the rivers, the mighty Fraser River alone can pump 2.6 million gallons (10 million L) of water each second into the Salish Sea. Imagine 60,000 bathtubs of water pouring out every second! In this photo, you can see the winter runoff billowing like a cloud of smoke from the Fraser River into the Salish Sea.

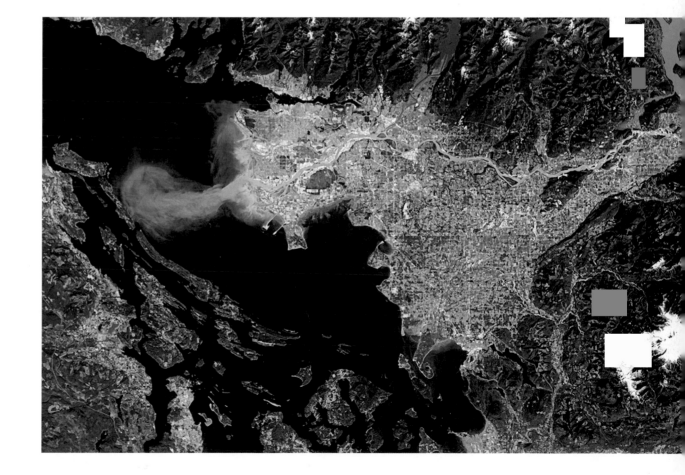

Sunlight is the major source of energy on land *and* in the ocean. No matter how much oxygen and nutrients are in the Salish Sea, without sunlight there would be no life. On land, plants are the primary producers of energy. In the Salish Sea, microscopic *phytoplankton* play that role. These floating single-cell organisms collect the sun's energy. Through a process called *photosynthesis*, they use the sun's rays as an energy source to grow—just like plants on land do. Phytoplankton are then eaten by other plankton called *zooplankton*, which are eaten by other larger organisms. The food web eventually grows into a massive complicated tangle of who-eats-whom that ultimately includes every creature in the ecosystem.

Snow-capped mountain ranges, the perfect blend of freshwater and saltwater, ample sunlight, and microscopic phytoplankton combine to support an inland sea filled with 38 mammals, 172 birds, 253 fish, 2 reptiles, and more than 3,000 macroinvertebrate species. You won't find another place like the Salish Sea . . . anywhere.

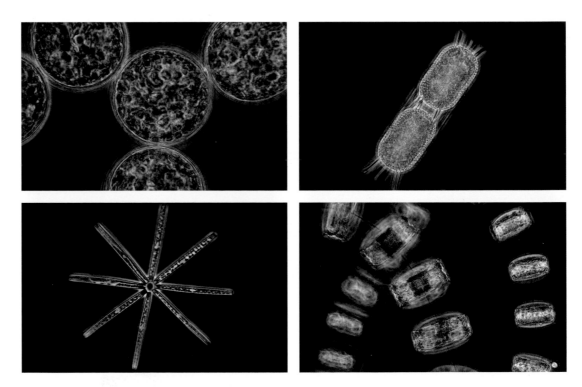

A sea soup of Salish Sea plankton as viewed through a microscope.

THE LAND-SEA CONNECTION

You might not realize how many species living on land depend on the Salish Sea. For example, the American dipper (top right) never visits the sea but feeds on aquatic insects that live in fast-moving streams that drain into the Salish Sea. Eggs (like you see in this dipper's beak) laid by salmon returning from the Salish Sea are also an important food for dippers. In fact, the American dipper is one of over 138 vertebrate species that rely on salmon as part of their diet. Bears (top left) and eagles (bottom) are other examples of animals that depend on salmon and on the Salish Sea.

Although the stones
on the beach are
extraordinarily diverse,
each one tells a different
chapter in the geologic
history of the Salish Sea.

BEACHCOMBING ALONG THE SHORES of the Salish Sea is like climbing aboard a geologic time machine. Almost no one can resist picking up a surf-polished rock and admiring its colors and patterns. Each rock on the beach represents a different chapter in the geologic history of the Salish Sea. The beach is just their latest stop on a journey that began millions of years ago.

Learning to identify and "read" the rocks will help you understand the geologic events that created the Salish Sea. A rock's appearance tells you whether it came from deep within the Earth or was formed closer to the surface out of magma that erupted from a volcano. You might even be lucky enough to find a rock with fossil shells in it and know that millions of years ago your rock was part of an ancient ocean seafloor. The detective work involved in finding out how a particular rock fits into the Salish Sea's geologic history is like solving a mystery!

Wind and wave action sculpted this sandstone into a honeycomb-like pattern.

MISSION: ROCK DETECTIVE!

ANDESITE PORPHYRY (V)
SANDSTONE (S)
AGATE (QUARTZ MINERAL)
BASALT (V)
HORNBLENDE SCHIST (M)

MARBLE (M)
QUARTZ VEINS (MINERAL)

RHYOLITE PORPHYRY (V)
MUDSTONE (S)

BRECCIA (V)

GRANODIORITE & DIORITE (I)
OLIVINE BASALT (V)
ANDESITE PORPHYRY (V)
QUARTZ (MINERAL)

GRANITE PORPHYRY (I)

SANDSTONE (S)

QUARTZ VEINS (MINERAL)

GRANITE (I)
GNEISS (M)

JASPER (QUARTZ MINERAL)

KEY   I = Igneous (intrusive)   V = Igneous (volcanic/extrusive)   M = Metamorphic   S = Sedimentary

Rocks are made up of different minerals, which determine color and appearance. Geologists classify rocks into three groups—*igneous, sedimentary*, and *metamorphic*—based on how they formed.

IGNEOUS rocks form from *magma* (or lava) that flows up from deep within the Earth, cooling and solidifying at great depth or near/at the surface. There are two types of igneous rocks—*intrusive* and *extrusive*. Intrusive igneous rocks, like granite, form when magma cools and hardens deep underground. Slower cooling produces larger crystals; faster cooling produces small- to medium-size crystals. Extrusive (volcanic) igneous rocks, such as basalt, form when magma erupts from a volcano or solidifies in a volcanic chamber just beneath the Earth's surface. The quickest cooling of all results in glass-like rocks, such as obsidian. Some volcanoes are very explosive, erupting superhot clouds of volcanic ash and rock fragments that cool quickly and form rocks, such as pumice and tuff.

SEDIMENTARY rocks form on the Earth's surface when layers of sediment (sand, mud, gravel) accumulate and become cemented together over time to form rocks like sandstone or mudstone. Sedimentary rocks resemble the places where they formed. A sandstone rock you find may once have been a sandy beach, the mudstone an ancient mudflat, and the limestone a muddy, shell-rich seafloor.

METAMORPHIC rocks start out as igneous or sedimentary rocks. When mountain-building or other geologic events bury these preexisting rocks deep within the Earth, they undergo complete *metamorphosis* (or change) resulting from the extreme pressure and heat of deep burial. Melting and recrystallizing at depth, the new rock has all the same minerals but looks entirely different from the original. Examples include gneiss (from granite), quartzite (from sandstone), and marble (from limestone).

TOP: Be glad you weren't a scuba diver exploring the Cretaceous-age Salish Sea 100 million years ago, when the ocean was filled with giant swimming *ammonites* capturing and crushing prey with their powerful tentacles. Ammonites, shelled relatives of octopuses and squid, ranked among the top predators in the oceans for nearly 300 million years. These amazing animals went extinct about 65 million years ago, at the end of the Cretaceous, when a comet struck the Earth. Ammonite fossils (like the ones pictured here) are found on just a few islands in the Salish Sea. The best sites are on Sucia Island (San Juan Islands), Hornby Island (Canadian Gulf Islands), and on the eastern side of Vancouver Island. Most ammonite fossils, as well as *baculites* (small squid-like creatures) and giant clams, are found in the limestone sedimentary rocks that formed at the bottom of the ancestral Pacific Ocean at least 60 to 90 million years ago.

BOTTOM: Glaciers often carry huge boulders, called *erratics*, that are left behind when the glacial ice melts. It's easy to identify an erratic because it is often rounded and isn't like any of the other rocks or outcrops nearby. The granite erratics in this photo probably came from the Coast Range in British Columbia, where you'll find the largest granite outcropping in the world.

The amazing geologic forces that gave birth to the Salish Sea began about 200 million years ago. The ocean basins that make up our inland sea and the mountain ranges and volcanoes that surround its shores are the result of *plate tectonics*, a geologic phenomenon that begins deep within the Earth. Let's take a look at how plate tectonics work.

The Earth's outermost crust, the *lithosphere*, is broken into several huge oceanic and continental plates and many smaller plates. The Earth's continents and oceans are situated on these rigid rock plates, which "float" on top of the semisolid rock layer known as the *upper mantle*. Heat and magma flowing upward from the Earth's core are what force the crustal plates to move—and they are still moving today! Whenever plates are moving apart, sliding past each other, or colliding, they create mountains, cause volcanic eruptions, and trigger earthquakes.

The Pacific/Juan de Fuca Plate (*oceanic*) and the westward-moving North American Plate (*continental*), the plate on which we live, have been colliding for millions of years to create the Salish Sea. The boundary between these two plates is defined by a very active 620-mile (1,000-km) fault, the Cascadia, which extends from northern California to northern Vancouver Island. Where the two plates collide, the Juan de Fuca Plate plunges beneath the North American Plate and into the mantle, where it periodically triggers earthquakes, forces magma to rise toward the surface to erupt from volcanoes, and adds new rock to the bases of mountain ranges all along the Salish Sea's easternmost shores.

Washington's Mount Baker, just like Mount Rainier and Canada's Mount Garibaldi, is one of several volcanoes that you can see along the mainland shores of the Salish Sea.

Clouds fill the mountain valleys of
the Cascades like converging rivers
of glacial ice once did during the
Pleistocene Ice Age.

Over millions of years, the Salish Sea's mountain ranges, created by plate tectonics, grew in height and acted like a dam, capturing moisture from clouds flowing eastward from the Pacific Ocean. The increased moisture changed the climate all along the western slopes of the mountains and created a network of streams, rivers, and the evergreen forests—the watersheds that now deliver freshwater and nutrients to the Salish Sea.

During the Pleistocene era, a geologic time beginning about 1.8 million years ago, the climate became colder and giant ice caps formed in the highest mountains. The colossal Cordilleran ice sheet grew and flowed southwestward from British Columbia and into western Washington. It merged with huge glaciers flowing out of the Coast Range, the Cascades, and the Olympics. By 20,000 years ago, these glaciers covered much of the Salish Sea.

Climatic warming brought the Salish Sea's deep freeze to an end. The Cordilleran ice sheet melted and retreated. About 10,000 years ago, Puget Sound, the Strait of Juan de Fuca, and the Strait of Georgia were completely ice-free, and for the first time they formed an interconnected inland sea—the Salish Sea we know today.

The same geologic forces—plate tectonics and Ice Age glaciers—that created what we see on land also created a complex world beneath the Salish Sea. The seafloor's *geodiversity* (or geologic diversity) is important because it provides a dazzling variety of habitats for marine plants and animals. The Salish Sea's extraordinary biodiversity is a result of its geodiversity.

A starry flounder lies buried in sand left by melting glaciers.

During the Pleistocene era, glacial ice was nearly 8,000 feet (2,400 m) thick above what is now Vancouver, British Columbia. It was 6,000 feet (1,800 m) thick over Bellingham, Washington, and 3,000 feet (900 m) thick above Seattle—about the height of five Space Needles stacked on top of each other!

These mountains were sculpted by glaciers.

Life at the Edges:
The Intertidal World

ALONG THE EDGES OF THE SALISH SEA, plants and animals have adapted to life where sea level is constantly rising or falling. The shore area exposed between high tide and low tide is called the *intertidal zone*. The twice daily *ebb* (or outflow of water) and *flood* (or inflow of water) of the tides shape the rhythm of life in this narrow band of shoreline.

The oxygen that most marine animals need to survive is dissolved in seawater, so when the tide is out, they must keep their body tissues moist by burrowing into wet sand or mud, or by seeking shelter beneath rocks and kelp. At low tide, when there is little or no food available for intertidal invertebrates, they must alternate between periods of activity and biding their time until the flood tide delivers food and oxygen with every incoming wave. For us and for other land animals that hunt for food in the intertidal zone, the Coast Salish have a saying: "When the tide is out, the table is set."

FAST CURRENTS

When you place your finger partially over the end of a hose, a dribble of water becomes a fast-moving spray. Tides act in the same way. They push water through narrow channels of land and force the water to speed up. These fast currents can reach speeds of 16 knots (30 km/hr) at Skookumchuck Narrows in British Columbia—more than two times the top speed for most sailboats, which may frustrate those wishing to sail against the tide. For expert kayakers, strong tides create playgrounds of fast-moving water.

Tides, creators of the intertidal zone, are controlled by the sun's and the moon's gravitational pulls on the Earth. Along with the wind and the estuarine circulation (mixing freshwater and saltwater), they also push huge volumes of water through the sea, mixing nutrients and oxygen, and carrying microscopic juvenile forms of fish and invertebrates (called *larvae*) from their birth sites. Powerful tidal currents can also force fish, like herring, to swim in certain directions, and, at times, push boats and scuba divers in directions they may or may not want to go.

The Salish Sea boasts many types of intertidal habitats. *Habitat* includes the community of animals and plants that live there and the physical conditions that determine how these species must adapt to survive. This includes the type of soil or rocks, plants, and the presence, absence, or intermittent presence of water. Common intertidal habitats you can find in the Salish Sea include tidal flats, rocky shorelines, and eelgrass.

Tidal flats are created when an ebbing tide leaves a flat area of sand or mud. From a distance, mudflats may look boring and without life. Take a closer look and you will see holes, mounds, and corkscrew-shaped piles that tell you that there is a whole different world beneath the surface. A great diversity of burrowing invertebrates and fish species use tidal flats as habitat during some portion of their life cycle.

Next time you visit a tidal flat, use your hand or a small trowel to dig into the mud and see what you can find. You might find burrowing mud shrimp, clams, oysters, snails, or crabs. Unless you use a microscope, you will not be able to see the tiny *diatoms* (or single-celled phytoplankton) that cover the surface of mudflats and create nutritious fuel for small migrating birds. This supersmoothie is called *biofilm*.

Tiny shorebirds called Dunlin use their long bills to probe for food on a mudflat.

GHOSTLY SHRIMP AND FORMIDABLE GRAY WHALES

While digging in a mudflat at low tide, you might find a ghoulish-looking pink and white crustacean, the well-named ghost shrimp. These large shrimp may look frightening, but they're harmless. They spend their days digging long branching burrows in the mud and, when the tide comes in, filtering *detritus* (or dead organic material) from the water, all while trying to avoid being eaten by a gray whale.

The gray whale, which can be longer than a school bus, is a formidable hunter of small invertebrates. Armed with a 2,500-pound (1,100-kg) tongue that can create suction, and with baleen in its upper jaw for a filter, it waits for the tide to come in over the mud, swims in, scoops up, filters out, and eats the ghost shrimp.

Black oystercatchers often can be found walking along rocky shorelines where they use their sturdy, long red bills to eat limpets and mussels—but not oysters. Perhaps it should have been named the black limpetcatcher or the black musseleater?

Exposed rock, low-growing kelp, strong currents, and extreme tidal action characterize *rocky shorelines*, another intertidal habitat. At low tide these are great locations to search for intertidal invertebrates, especially in *tide pools*, which are small pools of water that remain at low tide. High in the intertidal zone you may find tiny barnacles escaping predation by crabs and sea stars. Lower in the zone you'll find multiple species of crabs, sea stars, limpets, anemones, worms, and even small eel-shaped fish.

Eelgrass is a plant that creates another type of intertidal habitat that resembles an undersea prairie. Its slender algae-coated leaves offer places where fish, crabs, and other invertebrates can live, feed, and hide.

Some fish species live in eelgrass meadows only when they are young. Others live there as adults too. Huge schools of Pacific herring use these meadows for *spawning* (or laying their eggs) on the eelgrass. When the young hatch, they are in a relatively safe place to begin growing up. It's "relatively safe" because eelgrass not only supports the creatures that live in these meadows but also provides feeding grounds for the fish, birds, and mammals that come there to hunt.

Many species of blood stars (top) can be found intertidally throughout the Salish Sea, even in or near eelgrass meadows. Unlike the blood star, which stands out, the bay pipefish (bottom) is an excellent mimic of the eelgrass in which it lives. It is colored, shaped, and moves with the current like eelgrass. Camouflage helps fish hide from predators and, at times, from the animals they are hunting.

SHORELINE PREDATORS

The shorelines of the Salish Sea are a rich buffet of kelp, fish, and invertebrates for birds and land-based mammals like this mink (bottom). As you explore, you may also see crows, belted kingfishers, and a variety of gulls, as well as river otters (top), raccoons, black-tailed deer, and maybe even a black bear.

MISSION: INTERTIDAL

RIGHT: You can be an intertidal explorer. Find a field guide for the seashore and a tide table for your local beach and go! When you arrive, you might not notice anything. Wait and watch. You will begin to see fish and crabs moving in tide pools. Gently turn over rocks smaller than your hand (any larger and you might kill animals hiding below) and look for creatures hiding beneath or clinging to the bottom of the rock.

Be gentle as you look for tidal creatures; they have to survive some extremely difficult living conditions. In the Salish Sea, the lowest daytime tides occur in the hottest summer months, and the lowest nighttime tides are in the coldest winter months. This means intertidal animals have to survive being exposed on the year's hottest days and the coldest nights.

When you find something, your first task is to identify it by name. Then learn how it lives, what it eats, who might eat it, how it moves, and how it survives being exposed to such extreme conditions.

To be sure the creatures survive, gently return the rock to its original position when you are done exploring.

Life in the Deep:
The Subtidal World

MOST PEOPLE SEE THE SALISH SEA from a beach or a boat, but only a small group of explorers actually venture beneath the water into the *subtidal zone*, which is the area deeper than the intertidal zone that is never exposed to the air.

The water there is cold, deep, and dark; the currents can be swift; and you have to bring your own air. Let's take a "dive" beneath the surface of the Salish Sea and learn about some of its wildest and best-kept secrets.

Diversity reigns supreme over the subtidal invertebrates in the Salish Sea. You can find animals in every shape, size, and color you can imagine—probably even a few you can't. There may be more than 3,000 invertebrate species in the Salish Sea, and those are only the ones you can see without a microscope.

Their bold coloration, like the opalescent nudibranch (left), red flabellina (top right), and the giant nudibranch shown laying eggs (bottom right), sends a warning: *Beware! I'm poisonous.*

The Salish Sea is home to many record holders: world's largest barnacle (giant barnacle), largest burrowing clam (geoduck), largest chiton (gumboot chiton), and largest octopus (giant Pacific octopus). It is also a worldwide hot spot for almost 30 species of sea stars, many with 5 arms, but some with 8, 10, 11, 12, or even 16. One, the sunflower star (right), can have up to 24 arms, weigh 11 pounds (5 kg), and measure 4 feet (1.2 m) across. It is huge and is considered the largest sea star in the world.

What you find in the subtidal zone depends on where you go. Different habitats support different species. Sunlight rarely reaches deeper than 65 feet (20 m), so if you were to dive deeper, you wouldn't find algae, plants, or plankton, which depend on photosynthesis to survive. Creatures of the deep are mostly predators that have adapted to living and hunting in the dark. Predators eating other predators—talk about a dark underworld!

Like light and ocean depth, the *substrate* (or material) that forms the seafloor varies and creates different kinds of habitat. Where the seafloor is sandy, tidal currents can create underwater sandstorms, which make sand waves that can tower nearly 100 feet (30 m) high. That's as tall as a ten-story building!

You won't find filter-feeding invertebrates in these sandy areas because they would become buried and die. Instead you might find thousands of Pacific sand lance burrowed in the sand dunes, hiding from predators. These fish are able to breathe even beneath the sand, preferring to bury in larger-grained sand that allows oxygen to penetrate to their gills.

A buried spear-shaped Pacific sand lance emerges from its sandy hideout.

In subtidal rocky habitats where there are no sand waves, filter-feeding invertebrates, such as giant barnacles and anemones, may spend their entire lives anchored to the same rock. The strong currents that prevent sand or mud from settling on the rocks and burying these stationary creatures also deliver a steady supply of plankton as food.

Many of these invertebrates have really long life spans. The red urchin, for example, can live to be 150 years old. Imagine hanging on to a rock for that many years and catching and eating the rare piece of kelp that drifts by. The only thing less exciting might be the life of a geoduck, which buries itself into the mud and can live there for as long as 168 years.

In shallow, rocky subtidal habitat where light is abundant, you'll usually find lots of different types of kelp, a brown algae seaweed that attaches to the rocky seafloor. In fact, nearly two dozen species of kelp grow in the Salish Sea. Bull kelp and giant kelp have floats that keep most of the plant at or near the surface of the water, so they get maximum light for photosynthesis. The *stipes* (or stalks) of the kelp form an undersea forest. Kelp forests shelter a multitude of invertebrates and fish.

Much to the delight of scuba divers (and sea lions), there is great variety among the rocky reefs and kelp forests of the Salish Sea.

Diving in an undersea forest of bull kelp allows you to move between huge blades of kelp in three dimensions and pass untold numbers of interesting creatures, like this Puget Sound king crab, that live there. It must be what it feels like to be a bird flying through a tropical rainforest.

More than 250 species of fish can be found in the Salish Sea. They vary from tiny camouflaged sculpins, which are rarely seen because they blend in so well, to the giant 30-foot (9-m) basking sharks, which are the second-largest fish in the world.

The Salish Sea is lucky to have all five species of Pacific salmon running wild in its waters. But plenty of less famous fish call it home too. There's the Pacific spiny lumpsucker, the longsnout prickleback, the bigeye poacher, the giant wrymouth, and the hagfish, just to name a few. Their names may not be as well known as salmon, but they are definitely much funnier.

After being guarded by their mother for 6 to 7 months, young octopuses begin to hatch (left). As hatchlings (right), they look like miniature versions of adult octopuses.

AN OCTOPUS'S GARDEN . . . OR GUARD DEN?

A female giant Pacific octopus can lay up to 100,000 eggs. She'll guard and care for these eggs in her den, often found in rocky habitats, for up to a year until they hatch, after which the mother dies. Newly hatched planktonic larvae are as small as grains of rice but still look like adult octopuses. They float in the water for 4 to 6 weeks and can travel great distances before they settle out of the water and change into bottom-dwelling animals.

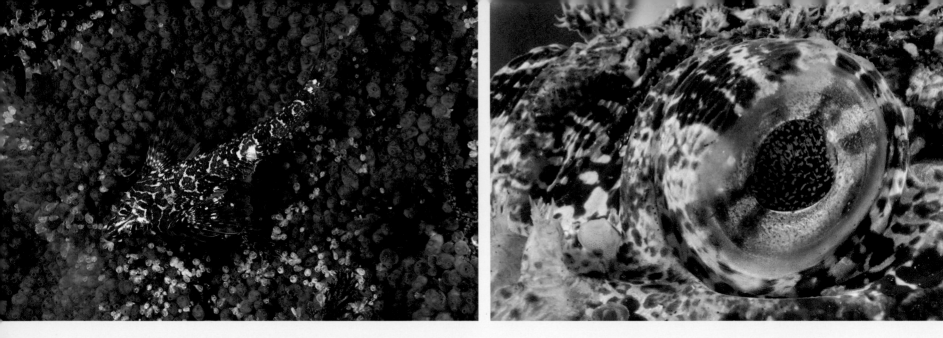

SCULPINS: MASTERS OF CAMOUFLAGE

Sculpins rely on camouflage to hide from their prey and from their predators. Even the eyes of this red Irish lord (top right) are camouflaged. Can you find the sculpin in each photo?

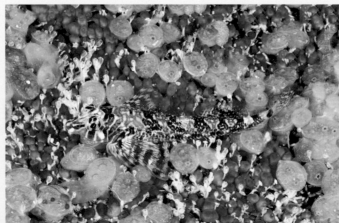

CRAZY FISH

With so many different fish species in the Salish
Sea, it is no surprise that they come in many crazy
shapes and sizes, and do crazy things. Some, like the
decorated warbonnet (top left), have so many *cirri*
(or projections) coming from their head and dorsal
fin spines that they appear to be wearing feathered
headgear traditionally worn by American Plains
Indians. Markings on others, like the gunnel (left), are
more subtle and allow them to blend in to their kelp
surroundings. With their large heads, the jowls of a wild
boar, and a mouth full of sharp teeth, wolf eels (top
right) are one of the few fishes capable of crushing
spiny red urchins with a single bite.

HOW FISH BREATHE UNDERWATER AND HOW WE CAN TOO!

A fish can breathe underwater because as water enters its mouth, it passes over the fish's *gills* (the fish equivalent of lungs) that sit behind its mouth, where molecules of oxygen are taken into the fish's blood. This process is much like ours when we are on land. Air enters our mouths and travels to our lungs, where oxygen molecules pass across a fine layer of tissue and into our blood.

Since we can't extract oxygen from water like fish, we have to take air with us in a self-contained underwater breathing apparatus—also known by the acronym SCUBA—when exploring the undersea world. Scuba divers are able to breathe from a tank filled with compressed air, giving them a rare glimpse into the undersea world of the Salish Sea.

Mosshead warbonnet

FINDING A HOME

In the subtidal zone, piles of rocks (top right), shells of long-dead barnacles (bottom right), or even a discarded bottle (left) are hiding places for fish or their eggs.

Wolf eels

Fish eggs

A humpback whale surfaces with a mouthful of herring. Can you find the rhinoceros auklet resting patiently in the background?

Chapter 6
Life Between Two Worlds: Diving Birds and Mammals

DIVING SEABIRDS AND MAMMALS breathe air like us, but spend much of their life underwater holding their breath. If humans had to do that, it would present serious problems. But these animals are adapted for life between two worlds: the land and the sea. They can stay submerged underwater longer than we can because they are able to store oxygen in their muscles in the same way we store food in a refrigerator. It's there when it's needed.

The molecule we need in the air we breathe is oxygen. Your muscles need oxygen to work. If you do not bring new oxygen through your mouth into your lungs and to your muscles through your bloodstream, your muscles quickly run out of oxygen. Diving birds and mammals don't have to worry about this.

A Pacific white-sided dolphin prepares to surface, exhaling just before reaching the surface and taking in a new breath of air.

Minke whale breaching

MISSION: BREATH-HOLDING CHALLENGE

How long can you hold your breath? Try it. Were you able to last an entire minute? Check out the dive duration records for some of the Salish Sea's diving birds and mammals and see how you compare.

Pigeon guillemot	2 minutes, 24 seconds
Rhinoceros auklet	2 minutes, 30 seconds
Common murre	3 minutes, 32 seconds
Harbor porpoise	5 minutes, 21 seconds
Pacific white-sided dolphin	6 minutes, 12 seconds
Killer whale	11 minutes, 12 seconds
Harbor seal	32 minutes, 30 seconds
Northern elephant seal	77 minutes

We breathe not only to take in oxygen but also to get rid of a molecule called carbon dioxide (CO_2). It is the build-up of CO_2 in our bodies that makes us want to take a breath. But diving birds and mammals can tolerate much greater levels of CO_2 than we can, so they don't "feel" the need to breathe as quickly as we do.

These diving animals also need to easily travel through water, which is harder than traveling through air. Because water is 784 times more *dense* (or thick) than air, it makes sense that moving through this denser world requires more energy than we are used to. Have you have ever tried running in waist-deep water? If so, you understand! Fortunately, diving birds and mammals have sleek shapes that let them move through water more easily.

Porpoising Pacific white-sided dolphins

Diving marine birds and mammals need powerful propulsion mechanisms and sleek shapes to push themselves forward. Have you ever looked closely at a harbor seal? Its tubular form comes from having most of its hind legs incorporated into its rocket ship–like design. Its large webbed feet are the only part that sticks out from its body. The seal uses its front feet like miniwings to steer, while its large webbed hind feet are held straight back. It glides from side to side to accelerate. This side-to-side movement is similar to what most fish do.

A whale's body is slightly different. Evolution has left whales completely without hind legs, which gives them their smooth form but takes away an important source of power. But this doesn't mean whales aren't powerful! Fortunately, they have large tails, called *flukes*. Rather than using a side-to-side motion to swim like a seal, a whale arches its body and powerful tail in an up-and-down movement to propel itself.

A third form of propulsion can be found in sea lions and humpback whales, which have very long *pectoral fins* (or front flippers). They use these fins like a bird uses its wings to "fly" through the water.

TOP: Underwater, a harbor seal shows its tubular form and use of its front flippers like miniwings to steer.

MIDDLE/BOTTOM: The humpback whale uses its powerful tail and long pectoral fins (arms) to help breach out of the water and to propel itself through the water.

Like marine mammals, diving birds use their feet or their wings (or both) to swim or fly through the water. Look at these pictures of a diving bird and a mammal. Can you guess which parts of their anatomy help them get through the water?

All these adaptations mean that diving birds and mammals can explore the Salish Sea at depths we humans can barely imagine. Scuba divers descend 120 feet (37 m), but common loons and long-tailed ducks can dive to more than 200 feet (61 m), common murres and Dall's porpoises to 590 feet (180 m), and harbor seals to an astounding 1,630 feet (500 m).

Imagine you are a harbor seal diving to 1,000 feet deep. You would feel a great amount of pressure on your body from all that water, *and* you wouldn't be able to see anything. That's right, it is pitch-black at that depth. Fortunately, harbor seals have highly specialized whiskers that enable them to "fish" without using their eyes. Their whiskers can sense the track a fish leaves behind while swimming through the water a full 30 seconds after the fish has passed, much like a tracker dog can pick up the scent of a person long after the person has walked by. The seal senses the fish's path and pursues it, eventually catching dinner without ever seeing it.

Living below the water as an air-breathing bird or mammal is challenging, yet many air-breathing animals have evolved in ways to survive underwater. Their adaptations are truly something to marvel over.

A rhinoceros auklet uses its wings to "fly" underwater.

Steller sea lions use their hind and fore flippers to power through the water.

THE ACOUSTIC WORLD OF ODONTOCETES

Odontocetes—or toothed whales, such as dolphins, porpoises, and killer whales—communicate, navigate, and find food through the use of sound. Specifically, they are able to send out sound waves and use the *echo* (or sounds that bounce back) to create a mental image like we do with light that enters our eyes. This ability, called *echolocation*, helps them navigate in deep, dark places with low visibility.

Chapter 7
Epic Journeys

THE PACIFIC OCEAN AND THE SALISH SEA are connected by more than the water that flows between them. A variety of animals also migrate to and from the Salish Sea and tell the story of how it is connected to the global ocean. These journeys are not only epic feats of athletic adventure but border on sheer magic. It does, after all, seem supernatural that survival for so many fish, birds, and mammals depends on traveling thousands upon thousands of miles to find food or reproduce.

The migration made by salmon is one of the world's most famous. Born in the farthest reaches of small freshwater mountain streams, salmon migrate downriver into the salty Salish Sea and out to the open ocean. As adults, they will eventually return to that same stream to spawn, depositing eggs and sperm that will become the next generation of salmon. Finding the exact stream in which they were born after living in the ocean for 3, 4, or even 6 years is an amazing accomplishment. This monumental migration is even more incredible if you realize that during those years in the ocean, most salmon travel as far north as Alaska or as far west as Japan before returning to the Salish Sea and then, ultimately, to the stream where they were born— their *natal stream*.

Sockeye salmon in the Fraser
River stack up like cordwood
as they return to spawn.

DINING IN DANGEROUS PLACES

Small worms and other invertebrates are only a fraction of the diet of migrating western sandpipers. At some locations almost half of their diet comes from biofilm, a thin layer of goo that forms on the surface of intertidal mudflats.

Biofilm is mostly made of microscopic plankton (diatoms) mixed in with other organisms. Stopping to fatten up on this nutritious goo is risky, however. A hungry peregrine falcon knows that hundreds of thousands of sandpipers will feed close to shore where biofilm is most abundant. It's a dangerous location, but the hungriest sandpipers are usually the skinniest, which enables them to take off quickly and easily if a peregrine swoops in.

As the sandpipers fatten, their takeoff speed slows, so they choose to eat at a location farther from shore. You can watch this complex struggle between hungry falcons and hungry sandpipers every spring and fall.

Like salmon, gray, humpback, minke, and killer whales also migrate in and out of the Salish Sea to the global ocean.

Some individual gray whales live year-round in the Salish Sea. But most migrate each year between the Pacific coastal lagoons of Baja California and the cold, food-rich waters of Alaska. During the winter, gray whale mothers give birth to their young in the shallow warm water lagoons of Mexico, and then mother and calf (as seen below) travel north together to spend the summer on an Arctic feeding spree, where they fatten up before making the 9,000-mile (14,500-km) migration back to Mexico.

Imagine swimming from Mexico to Alaska with a newborn. This demanding journey is made even more challenging by killer whales intent on eating the newborn gray whale calves along the way.

For tiny shorebirds, migrating between the Alaskan and Canadian Arctic and places as far south as Tierra del Fuego (at the tip of South America) is no small feat. Migrating shorebirds can't carry food with them, so their survival absolutely depends on stopping at food-rich sites along the way to refuel.

The Salish Sea's tidal flats and bays provide some of the most important stopover sites for migratory shorebirds along the entire Pacific flyway, a north–south superhighway for migratory birds that follows the western coast of North and South Americas. These giant intertidal mudflats loaded with burrowing shrimp, snails, and crabs are like giant all-you-can-eat buffets for the migrants.

Without places in the Salish Sea like Alice Bay, Boundary Bay, False Bay, Roberts Bank, and the Skagit River delta, just to name a few, the intercontinental migrations of more than 30 species of shorebirds could cease to exist. Hundreds of thousands of western sandpipers (right), least sandpipers, dunlins, Hudsonian godwits, long-billed dowitchers, semipalmated plovers, and black turnstones stop at these Salish Sea sites each spring and fall. Although they may stay only a week or so, the Salish Sea is as important to their survival as it is for the animals that spend their entire lives here.

THERE IS NO SUCH THING AS A SEAGULL

When you are walking on the beach you often hear people say, "Look, a seagull." But there is *no such thing as a "seagull."* There are, however, numerous species of gulls. The Salish Sea is home to 16 different gull species, including Bonaparte's, California, glaucous-winged, herring, mew, and Thayer's. Some species, like glaucous-winged gulls, are year-round residents. Others, like this Heermann's gull (left, seen with an anchovy in its bill), are seasonal visitors. Unlike many Salish Sea birds that migrate north in the summer to breed, Heermann's gulls migrate south in the winter to breed. Next time you see a gull foraging in the intertidal zone, remind yourself that it is not called a "seagull." Grab a field guide and see if you can figure out what species of gull it is.

Chapter 8
Be ■ Salish Se■ Hero

IF YOU LIVE NEAR THE SALISH SEA, you know it plays an important role in your life and the lives of everyone around you. It provides jobs, seafood, recreation, and inspiration. The mountains help create snow and rainfall, and the sea's stable water temperature shapes the mild climate of the region.

We all depend on the Salish Sea. Doesn't it make sense that we all should take care of it?

Unfortunately over the last 200 years we have done a terrible job of looking after the Salish Sea. We have cut down ancient forests in which some of the trees lived for 1,500 years guarding our shorelines. We have overfished, filled in tidal flats, dammed rivers, and dumped chemicals in the sea. It's not surprising that we have half as many salmon-eating killer whales as genetic studies show and only 5 percent of the salmon we had when the European explorers first ventured into the Salish Sea. What's more, fish and shellfish from some locations are no longer even safe to eat.

Western red cedar trees can live for 1,500 years and grow to more than 200 feet (61 m) tall. Before they were logged, old giants like the one seen here provided wildlife habitat, captured water, cooled streams, and protected newborn salmon.

By acting now, you can help reverse this trend and make the Salish Sea an even better place for us and for its plants and animals. First, respect the ocean like you respect yourself, your family, your friends, and your treasured possessions. We take care of what we care about. Next, take action!

A growing number of heroes are working to save the Salish Sea. Scientists are identifying reasons that fish, birds, and mammals are disappearing, and they are finding solutions to help bring them back. Biologists who manage wild food like salmon, Dungeness crab, and kelp are working to ensure we leave enough in the sea so that their populations will continue to reproduce and thrive, and we can harvest and enjoy them for generations to come. Elected officials are making laws that protect our ocean. Teachers and marine naturalist educators are teaching people about this unique place and inspiring them to help protect it.

You too can be a Salish Sea hero. Start a club that teaches your friends and other students about the Salish Sea. Volunteer with a group in your area that is working to restore a salmon-bearing stream. Write a letter to an elected official and let them know how important the Salish Sea is to all of us. Become a Junior SeaDoctor (it's free at SeaDocSociety.org) and join others like yourself who are taking steps to make a difference. Ask your friends, teachers, and parents to help you think of additional ways to help protect the Salish Sea. There is no shortage of things you can do.

SPECIES AT RISK

Many species that were once thriving in the Salish Sea (like the tufted puffin below) are in danger of disappearing—forever. Laws such as the Endangered Species Act (United States) and the Species at Risk Act (Canada) are meant to protect these animals and the places where they live. Scientists identify species that are at risk of extinction by looking at how animal populations change over time. Currently, almost 17 percent of fish, 34 percent of bird, and 43 percent of mammal species that live in the Salish Sea are listed as threatened or endangered or are candidates for listing. These numbers are too high, but you can play a part in bringing these species back.

Never be afraid that your actions are too small to matter. Every time you ride your bike or take public transportation instead of driving in a car, you reduce carbon dioxide emissions that contribute to ocean acidification, which is the ongoing decrease in ocean water pH caused by increases in CO_2 from the burning of fossil fuels. Even doing something as simple as picking up trash on the beach is a powerful start. The plastic strap you pick up today will not entangle a sea lion tomorrow.

The more actions you take, the more you can help the Salish Sea. Do something for this amazing place that does so much for all of us.

SAVING SEA LIONS

Carelessly discarded trash can entangle and kill a sea lion (left). Wildlife veterinarians and biologists (right) are working to safely free entangled animals, document types of trash causing the problem, and stop this problem at the source. Have you thought about pursuing a career that helps the Salish Sea?

Acknowledgments

Every book begins with an inspiration—ours came from elementary teachers and parents all around the Salish Sea who encouraged us to write a young reader's version of our award-winning book, *The Salish Sea: Jewel of the Pacific Northwest*. Neither of us had ever written a children's book, but we agreed that sharing our love for the Salish Sea with the next generation of Salish Sea enthusiasts, scientists, naturalists, and stewards was exactly what we needed to do.

We are profoundly grateful to Gary Luke, publisher of Sasquatch Books, for his unwavering belief in us and in the importance of this book. Our heartfelt thanks to our editor, Christy Cox, and her team at Little Bigfoot, the children's book imprint of Sasquatch Books, for their enthusiasm and expert guidance along the way. Once again, the collaborative partnership forged between Sasquatch Books, Cloud Ridge Publishing's team (especially the photographic vision of Wendy Shattil, Cloud Ridge's project manager and photo editor), and the combined fundraising efforts of our two nonprofits, the SeaDoc Society and Cloud Ridge Naturalists, enabled us to produce a book that we can all be proud of.

It is impossible for anyone to know everything about a place as diverse and marvelous as the Salish Sea. We thank the SeaDoc Society's science advisors and the other scientists and subject matter experts who provided scientific information, consultation, illustrations, and key concepts for inclusion in this book: E. Anderson, R. Butler, M. Chadsey, P. Chan, K. Currens, L. Dierauf, J. Donatuto, G. Greene, M. Haulena, G. Jensen, C. K. Johnson, T. Klinger, L. Lahner, K. Naish, J. Newton, J. Nichols, D. Noren, P. Ross, Seattle Aquarium staff, J. Smith, B. Swalla, Vancouver Aquarium staff, J. Watson, K. Wellman, J. West, and J. White.

We would also like to thank the numerous teachers, educators, and young readers who inspired us and who helped ensure that our content was not only age appropriate, but also exciting. Specifically we would like to call out: M. Briddell, K. Campion, B. Dahl, A. Kveven, S. Lundstrom, J. Lyle, L. Tidwell, and M. Van Lanen.

DONORS

This book would not have been possible without the generous financial support of the Benedict Family Foundation and matching gifts by SeaDoc Society supporters. Specifically, we would like to thank: C. and C. Abolin, T. Anderson and M. Cleveland, S. and R. Beaton, H. and L. Behar, A. Benedict, B. Bentley, B. and K. Bloemker, T. Bloemker Sowers and JC Sowers, M. Boero and V. Woodruff, B. Burns and S. Hiester, R. and B. Clever, M. Clure, R. and B. Cole, S. and C. Coleman, K. Dickinson, L. Dierauf and J. Hurley, J. and L. Donald, D. and L. Donner, R. and S. Donovan, D. Dotlich and D. Elwood, A. and J. Ebbeler, E. and J. Flath, J. and J. Fletcher, B. and S. Friel, K. and J. Gilardi, J. and L. Groban, W. and S. Gudgell, D. Harvell and C. Greene, J. and P. Henigson, L. Henry and P. Loew, the Margaret E. Johnson Family Fund, G. Krampf and P. King, K. Kuster and S. Moon, A. Kveven and K. Calvin, N. and K. Loomis, J. and K. Lufkin, S. and B. Mehlman, M. Mills, M. Murray, C. and L. Myhrvold, S. and L. Neal, L. and S. Newland, S. Peck and D. Gillespie, B. and C. Rakow, K. Ranker and T. Torri, I. Rasch, E. Rhodes, D. Roberts, B. Rosenkotter and T. Tyson, M. and J. Schneider, R. and C. Severson, T. and B. Stonecipher, K. Thornburgh and K. Rawson, D. Roberts, J. and R. Romines, S. Stoltz and D. Kau, D. Van Wie, B. Wareham, B. and M. Waunch, A. Weir and J. Bric, K. and K. Weisenburger, and P. and J. Wilson.

Photo Credits

p. i: Brandon Cole (top and bottom), Gerrit Vyn (middle) | p. ii: Marc Chamberlain | p. iv: Brandon Cole | p. v: Jared Towers | p. vi: Brandon Cole | p. vii: Marc Chamberlain (left), Brandon Cole (right) | p. viii: Geoff Hammerson | p. ix: Brett Baunton | p. 1: Les Bazso/Vancouver Sun | p. 2: Audrey Benedict | p. 3: ID 94778748, © Tomas Griger, Dreamstime.com | p. 4: Art Wolfe | p. 5: Brandon Cole | p. 6: Garth Lenz | p. 7: Brandon Cole | p. 8: Brandon Cole | p. 9: NASA | p. 10: Kathy Newell p. 11: Amy Gulick (top left and bottom), Glenn Bartley (top right), | p. 12: Ethan Welty (left), John D'Onofrio (right) | p. 13: Art Wolfe | p. 14: Wendy Shattil/Bob Rozinski p. 15: VPC Photo (top), Wendy Shattil/Bob Rozinski (bottom) | p. 16: John D'Onofrio | p. 17: Steph Abegg | p. 18: Brandon Cole (left) | p. 19: Ethan Welty | p. 20: Marc Chamberlain | p. 21: Neil Schulman p. 22: Gerrit Vyn | p. 23: Wendy Shattil/Bob Rozinski (top), Geoff Hammerson (bottom) | p. 24: John Lowman | p. 25: Brandon Cole | p. 26: Phil Green (top), Amy Gulick (bottom) | p. 27: Brandon Cole | p. 28: Brandon Cole | p. 29: Marc Chamberlain (top), Brandon Cole (bottom) | p. 30: Brandon Cole (top), NOAA (bottom) p. 31: Brandon Cole (top), Florian Graner (bottom) | p. 32: Brandon Cole | p. 33: Dale Saunders | p. 34: Marc Chamberlain | p. 35: Brandon Cole (top left and bottom), Marc Chamberlain (top right) | p. 36: Brandon Cole | p. 37: Marc Chamberlain (left and bottom right), Brandon Cole (top right) | p. 38: John Lowman | p. 39: Traci Walter p. 40: Jared Towers (left), Brandon Cole (right) | p. 41: Brandon Cole | p. 42: Geoff Hammerson (top), Jessica Newley (bottom) | p. 43: Brandon Cole | p. 44: Brandon Cole p. 46: Gerrit Vyn (left), Carlos Gagon (right) | p. 47: Tim Zurowski (left), Ken Archer (right) | p. 48: Brandon Cole | p. 49: Byrne, Whatcom Museum, #1975 p. 50: Ken Archer | p. 51: Wendy Szaniszlo (left), the Marine Mammal Center (right) | p. 53: Audrey Benedict

Index

Note: Page numbers in *italic* refer to photographs.

A

ammonites, *15*
apex predators, v

B

baculites, 15
biodiversity, 2, 18
biofilm, 22, 46
birds, x, *11*
    diving, viii, *viii*, *38*, 39–40, 42, *42*
    holding breath underwater, viii, 39–40
    in intertidal zone, 22, *22*, 24, 26, 46–47
    migrations of, 2, 46–47, *46*, *47*
    protecting, 50, *50*

C

cirri, *35*

D

density of water, 40
detritus, 23
diatoms, 22, 46
dolphins, *39*, 40, *40*, *43*

E

ebbing tide, 21, 22
echolocation, 43
ecotypes, iv
eelgrass, 22, 25, *25*
erratics, *15*
estuaries, 7–9, *9*, 22

F

fish, vii, *vii*, x, *38*
    breathing underwater, 36
    in intertidal zone, 22, 25, *25*
    protecting, 5, 50
    in subtidal zone, 30, *30*, 33, *34–37*
    See also salmon
flood tide, 21
flukes, 41
fossils, 13, *15*

G

geodiversity, 18
geology, 13–19
ghost shrimp, *23*
giant Pacific octopus, vi, *vi*, 30, 33, *33*
glaciers, *15*, *17*, 18, *19*
global ocean, 2, *3*, 45, 46

H

habitats, 18, 22, 25, 30, 31

I

igneous rocks, 14, *14*
inland sea, 7, 10, 16
invertebrates, vi, *vi*, x, *15*, 21, 22, *23*, 25, *25*, 26, *28*, 29–33, 46

K

killer whales, *iv*, v, 40, 43, 46, *48*, 49

L

larvae, 22, *33*
lithosphere, 16

M

macroinvertebrates, x, 10
magma (lava), 13, 14, 16
mammals, *26*, 39–43, 50
    See also sea lions; whales
map, x
metamorphic rocks, 14, *14*
migrations, *8*, *44*, 45–47
mudflats. See tidal flats

N

natal stream, 45

O

octopuses. See giant Pacific octopus
odontocetes, 43
orcas. See killer whales

P

pectoral fins, 41, *41*
photosynthesis, 10, 30, 31
plankton, 10, *10*, 22, 31, 46
plate tectonics, 16, 18

Q

quillback rockfish, vii, *vii*

R

rhinoceros auklets, viii, *viii*, *38*, 40, *42*
rocks, types of, 14, *14*
rocky shorelines, 22, 25

S

Salish Sea
    facts about, x
    as international border, 1, 5
    name of, 1–2
    protecting, *1*, 49–51
salmon, *5*, *8*, *11*, 33, *44*, 45, 49
scuba diving, *31–32*, 36, 42
sculpins, 33, *34*
sea lions, *31*, 41, *42*, 51, *51*
seagulls, 47, *47*
seals, 40, 41, *41*, 42
sedimentary rocks, 14, *14*, *15*
spawning, *8*, 25, *44*, 45
stipes (stalks), 31
substrate, 30

T

tidal flats (mudflats), 22, *22*, *23*, 46–47
tide pools, 25, 26, *27*
tides, 21–23, *21*, 26, 30

U

upper mantle, 16

V

volcanoes, 14, 16, *16*

W

water cycle, 2
watersheds, 6, 7–9, *9*, 18
whales, *23*, *38*, 40, 41, *41*, 43, 46, *46*
    See also killer whales

The **SEADOC SOCIETY**, a partner with Cloud Ridge Naturalists in publishing *Explore the Salish Sea*, is a science-based marine conservation program of the UC Davis School of Veterinary Medicine's Karen C. Drayer Wildlife Health Center. Based on Orcas Island, SeaDoc has been working to improve the health of the Salish Sea since 2001.

SeaDoc is committed to making this book available to teachers and students throughout the Salish Sea, regardless of economic status. We encourage science teachers to contact us to learn more about using this book as a tool for incorporating place-based learning in the classroom. We also encourage students to make a commitment to help the Salish Sea by becoming a Junior SeaDoctor for free.

 For more information about tools for teachers, scholarship support for books, and the Junior SeaDoctor program, visit SeaDocSociety.org

All royalties from this book will be donated to the SeaDoc Society and Cloud Ridge Naturalists.

The SeaDoc Society
People and science healing the sea

Cloud Ridge
Naturalists